WILMETTE PUBLIC LIBRARY

D0844491

Wilmette Public Library
1242 Wilmette Avenue
Wilmette, Il 60091
847-256-5025

# MORTAL
# TRASH

# MORTAL TRASH

---

*POEMS*

---

# Kim Addonizio

W. W. NORTON & COMPANY
*Independent Publishers Since 1923*
NEW YORK | LONDON

WILMETTE PUBLIC LIBRARY

Copyright © 2016 by Kim Addonizio

All rights reserved
Printed in the United States of America
First Edition

For information about permission to reproduce selections from this book,
write to Permissions, W. W. Norton & Company, Inc.,
500 Fifth Avenue, New York, NY 10110

For information about special discounts for bulk purchases, please contact
W. W. Norton Special Sales at specialsales@wwnorton.com or 800-233-4830

Manufacturing by RR Donnelley
Book design by JAM Design
Production manager: Lauren Abbate

Library of Congress Cataloging-in-Publication Data

Names: Addonizio, Kim, date. author.
Title: Mortal trash : poems / Kim Addonizio.
Description: First edition. | New York : W. W. Norton & Company, 2016.
Identifiers: LCCN 2016008753 | ISBN 9780393249163 (hardcover)
Classification: LCC PS3551.D3997 A6 2016 | DDC 811/.54—dc23 LC
record available at http://lccn.loc.gov/2016008753

W. W. Norton & Company, Inc.
500 Fifth Avenue, New York, N.Y. 10110
www.wwnorton.com

W. W. Norton & Company Ltd.
Castle House, 75/76 Wells Street, London W1T 3QT

1 2 3 4 5 6 7 8 9 0

811
ADDONIZIO,
K.

*for Aya, always*

_____

# CONTENTS

## THE SONNETS

## THOUSANDS OF TIMES THROUGHOUT THE DAY

# MORTAL
# TRASH

# WISHBONE

# SCRAPBOOK

This is me, depressed out of my mind,
frailing the banjo, spilling red wine

on the white
king-sized

luckily-hotel's-and-not-my-
goose down comforter, this is me

walking and waxing nostalgic through the girlish shadows
of tall palm trees, the déjà vus

flying through the scene
suddenly, like those three

unnameable and therefore beautiful white birds.
This is me as a slowly-tearing-itself-apart cloud

and marveling
at a fire palely and flamily

emerging from a bowl, wavering
up through stones of cobalt glass. The air

wavers back. This is me in love
with the beauty of blue glass in flames, this is me on drugs

prescribed by my doctor
as I try once more

———

to sneak into night's closely guarded city,
my hollow horse ready

to wreak my demons and Blue Morphos
on the citizens of my sleep. I am most

myself when flashing rapidly
my iridescent wings, drinking

the juice of fallen fruit. Then again
look for me under your bed

where the ugly premodern vampires
still hide. The undead and I are lying

in wait. We are very interested in you
though this is still me. We are unstable and true.

We believe in the one-ton rose
and the displaced toilet equally. Our blues

assume you understand
not much, and try to be alive, just as we do,

and that it may be helpful to hold the hand
of someone as lost as you.

# STRAY SPARKS

There goes the lightbulb filament—
another soul uploaded to the ether,
cigarette hissing in a plastic cup,
the party on the deck entering the hour
of ominous sounds in the woods. Maybe
wild animals, maybe lesser demons—
strewing the garbage, thieving chickens
and itty dogs, clawing at the sliding doors.
The crash cart is rolled from the room.
The daughter looks at her drunk father
slumped in a hospital chair. Something flowers
in the air above the bed but no one
can say what. Even with a full box of matches
no one can get the pilot relit;
the oven stays cold, but at least the burners work.
The meal is spoiled, but at least there's wine.
The party guests disappear one at a time
into the trees. The two who are left
take off their clothes together.
There goes a candle wick
into a sea of melted wax. For an instant
it flames on the surface. Hot lights above
the amusement pier, screams and laughter,
then everything's frozen solid.
Step out carefully. Take an ax.

# IDIOMS FOR RAIN

Wheelbarrows are falling in the Czech Republic
but in Wales, old ladies and sticks are landing
on the farms not yet carried off by owls,
knives and forks are clattering on the barns.
In the sky above New York City, one dark cloud
of dogs, one of feral cats, one of lawn gnomes
lined up with buckets, more clouds erupting
from their corncob pipes, the storm getting ready
to hammer the rooftop gardens and drive pigeons
into the arms of gargoyles. Gurgle. Gargle.
Some dragon is down with the flu, asking
*Who am I without my Kundalini breath, why*
*don't I have any friends, as soon as I'm better*
*I'm going to torch an elementary school.*
In Union Square, the vendors are packing up
peaches and artisanal cheeses, castles
and pawns are being disappeared from
the chess players' tables, shitty art reinstalled
in the museums of panel vans.
Umbrellas and hoodies, tarps on the carts
of the homeless hunkering down
while leaves skid around. In Greece
chair legs drive themselves into stone
and sink into the Aegean, but in Syria
chemical weapons are descending
meaning raining down like secretaries
and restaurant workers from the towers,
meaning metaphor is being abandoned
for the hell of the real, meaning what falls
from the sky keeps falling. *Feallan.* Fission.

Thermonuclear but not yet cobalt.
What the rain said to the wind was not
*You push and I'll pelt*
but *Let's see who can destroy the most flowers*
though it also may have said *Sometimes*
*I want to weep softly while you moan*
*over the seedlings.* In Germany it rains
puppies where once rained Walther bullets,
and in Denmark, shoemakers' apprentices
land softly on the earth, and set off to teach
whom they can.

# LIVES OF THE POETS

One stood among the violets
listening to a bird. One went to the toilet
and was struck by the moon. One felt hopeless
until a trumpet crash, and then lo,
he became a diamond. I have a shovel.
Can I turn it into a poem? On my stove
I'm boiling some milk thistle.
I hope it will turn into a winged thesis
before you stop reading. Look, I'm topless!
Listen: approaching hooves!
One drowned in a swimming pool.
One removed his shoes
and yearned off a bridge. One lives
with Alzheimer's in a state facility, spittle
in his white beard. It
turns out words are no help.
But here I am with my shovel
digging like a fool
beside the spilth and splosh
of the ungirdled sea. I can't stop.
The horses are coming, the thieves.
I still haven't found lasting love.
I still want to hear viols
in the little beach hotel
that's torn down and gone.
I want to see again the fish
schooling and glittering like a veil
where the waves shove
against the breakwater. Gone

is the girl in her white slip
testing the chill with one bare foot.
It's too cold, but she goes in, so
carefully, oh.

# PLASTIC

A bunch of it is floating somewhere
way out in the Pacific.
If your love is deeper than the ocean,
then the surface of your love is a swirl
of swill, toothbrushes and swizzle sticks
carried by the inevitable current:
someone comes saying *Oh oh shit baby baby*
then someone leaves the house key on the table
and sends a vaguely apologetic email.
Sunlight is bad for plastic. Imagine an Evian bottle
having a breakdown, getting eaten by a jellyfish
which is eaten by a bigger fish
which becomes a breaded, deep-fried rectangle
on a cafeteria tray. In an airport
you can eat with a metal fork
but the knife must be made of extruded polymers
to keep you from committing hara-kiri
as you return from delivering your lecture
on postmodern literary theory.
Back home, while you take your green canvas bag
to the store for beer and cereal,
the garbage in the ocean drifts, sidereal.
Think of the Earth as a big snow globe
floating in space, only the snow is really sticky
and doesn't melt, even when the atmosphere
sizzles with migraine. Here come those zigzag lights
and a sickening feeling. Make that sinking.
Party cup, fake fruit, heart souvenir.
Even if your love is brighter than the sun,

the ick of snow keeps falling.
Everyone feels a little tender
when stabbed with a fork.

# DIVINE

Oh hell, here's that dark wood again.
You thought you'd gotten through it—
middle of your life, the ogre turned into a mouse
and heart-stopped, the old hag almost done,
monsters hammered down
into their caves, werewolves outrun.
You'd come out of all that, into a field.
There was one man standing in it.
He held out his arms.
Ping went your iHeart
so you took off all your clothes.
Now there were two of you,
or maybe one, mashed back together
like sandwich halves,
oozing mayonnaise.
You lived on grapes and antidepressants
and the occasional small marinated mammal.
You watched the DVDs that dropped
from the DVD tree. Nothing
was forbidden you, so no worries there.
It rained a lot.
You planted some tomatoes.
Something bad had to happen
because no trouble, no story, so
*Fuck you*, fine, whatever,
here come more black trees
hung with sleeping bats
like ugly Christmas ornaments.
Don't you hate the holidays?
All that giving. All those windup

crèches, those fake silver icicles.
If you had a real one you could skewer
the big cursed heart of your undead love.
Instead you have a silver noodle
with which you must flay yourself.
Denial of pleasure,
death before death,
alone in the woods with a few bats
unfolding their creaky wings.

# APPLIED MATHEMATICS

Maybe we're all just integers.
The genes using us to multiply.
Marketing teams herding us into focus groups
and serving us antibiotic silage
before hammering a product
into our foreheads.
Twenty-three million American chickens,
two hundred sixty-nine a minute:
hot wings galore.
Subtract these killed and maimed civilians
from these retired generals.
Body counts. Dollars donated
to the ALS marathon,
Amnesty International,
Poetry Daily. Do you ever just
keep those printed address labels they send
and throw away the pitch letter?
Number of minutes since my last confession.
Number of polar bears stranded
on Arctic ice, degrees of warming
times new Cadillac Escalades.
Amount of change a panhandler collects
for a pint of Gilbey's gin
after walking four blocks,
eating one-half a scavenged hot dog,
and repeating his mantra
to eighty-seven pedestrians.
Number of brain cells asphyxiated
divided by number of tequila shots.
How many integers have you slept with,

did you used to keep a list?
When two integers mate,
another, smaller integer may appear,
crying, it seems, nonstop.

# WAYS TO GO

Suicide by tiger is one way.
Lose billions for investors
and apply box cutters to your wrists
is another. You can jump from a bridge
but you may live, paralyzed,
and if you don't
the crabs will slurp out your eyes
which will put a crimp in your ability
to find your shoes in the afterlife.
Who wants to go there anyway,
it's full of people you avoided
when you still knew how to breathe.
My friend says she wants to die
but who doesn't, sometimes?
Just today I was watching a home movie
delivered by the Ghost of Christmas Past.
Look, there's the ocean view from my old house!
There are all the friends I don't see anymore,
and my ex cleaning the stove,
and my teenage daughter saying *Kill me*
when I ask what I can do for her,
then stomping off to her room.
If I could kill myself and go back there I would.
Then again, murmurs the Ghost
of Christmas Future, your hair
looks so much better now.

# PARTY

I know we've just met and everything
but I'd really like to fall apart on you now.
I'd like to think you're the kind of person
who'd refill my glass all night, then pour me
shitfaced into your car and take me home with you
so I could regurgitate salmon and triple cream Brie
and chocolate strawberries into your toilet,
and then you'd cook me a little something—
I'd like to think you're the kind of person who cooks—
while I rambled incoherently about my loneliness.
I know we've just met but I feel like maybe
you'd feed me and tuck me into your big bed
and only touch me as you covered me with the comforter.
I feel like you own a comforter. I also somehow sense
that your family was extremely dysfunctional
in a way that differs from mine only in surface details,
like which person was the black hole
and which the distant, faint mark in space
that might have been a star. I feel all that.
I feel kind of, I don't know, like my inner space heater
and TV and washing machine are all going at once.
Do you own a coffee grinder?
I have an ice cube tray. The last ice disappeared
a few months ago, into the freezer mist.
I miss that ice but once the mist gets hold of it,
it's gone for good. Unrelenting mist. Many-headed
mist. Who knew mist had undone so many.
I feel like my underwear would fit in your silverware caddy.
It's just a feeling, though. I could be wrong about that.
Could you get me another drink now?

I think we have chemistry. I really need a lab partner.
Could I just, you know, let my molecules separate
while you keep an eye on the burner? The flame's kind of fickle.
Here's hoping it doesn't go out.

# INTRODUCTION TO POETRY

Psychiatrists are not poetic.
Neither is flatulence, or anything involving the intestines.
Breasts are more poetic than penises

or vaginas. Or sunsets.
But better a penis and a vagina than a sunset,
especially a sunset over the glittering ocean, over the craggy peaks.

Rainbows: not an especially good idea
unless your name begins with Elizabeth
and ends with Bishop, and you are referring not to a rainbow

but to oil in a little rented boat. Oil has become more poetic
than ever, due to its listing in the thesaurus
as a synonym for suffering. Which

is more poetic: legless child, drowning polar bear, heartless lover?
If your house was burning down,
would you save

    a) your grandmother,
    b) the Picasso,
    c) your latest poem, the best and truest one
    you've ever written, which you will revise
    to include an elegy for your grandmother,
    using a cubist metaphor?

For revision is poetic, though it seemeth not so.
For thou shalt use no archaic diction
lest ye be stoned. In the biblical sense of the word.

———

For I must tell you again and again
to show. For when you tell,
ye are as rainbows at sunset arching over the breasts

of beautiful women.
For your ignorance is vast
but I assure you mine is vaster.

For my selective serotonin reuptake inhibitor
rises in the night sky among the starry Fays.
For a poem should not be mean; it should be darling

as a lapdog, but never yap. A poem
should only open its trap to praise
and fuck anyone who says otherwise.

Do not use the word *fuck* gratuitously.
Come to think of it, the penis is perfectly poetic
if used thusly: O my mushroom, we are as microvilli

in the body of the world,
its bleary incandescence, its corporations' need
to dress us like skeletons and hoard all the candy.

The fucking shits. I love you so much, baby.
No one should say that in a poem.
Fuck. Shit. Love. Now write.

# SEASONAL AFFECTIVE DISORDER

Whoever came up with the acronym must have been happy
to think of everyone in winter walking around
saying "I have SAD" instead of "This time of year,
when the light leaves early and intimations of colder
hours settle over the houses like the great oppressive
oily scutes of a dragon's belly, I feel, I don't know,
a sense of ennui, a listlessness or lassitude
but more than that a definite undertow of dread
spreading over the waters of my already not-
exactly-sunny-to-begin-with soul, if one can even
speak of the soul anymore, which is part of the problem,
isn't it, I mean, how do I even know if I have one,
given that I'm essentially a secular humanist and missing
whatever constellation or holy Smurf guides people
through their lives, Jesus or Muhammad and then
either Muhammad's son or second-in-command
depending on who you thought was the true
successor, which is only one of the problems still being
worked out by wars and car bombings just
as similar problems were solved in earlier times by flambéing
people in public after rack-induced confessions, and if
there's no immortal soul that's soon (too soon if you
ask me) to be either whirled up to heaven
like a cow shining in a tornado or else hauled screaming
into the underworld like a pig to a scalding tank,
that is, if we just, you know, stop, the filament worn out
or shooting through the glass and exploding the bulb
but either way, done, done for, pure nothing, the socket empty
for long enough to hear some prayers or poems and then
another little lightbulb's screwed into place with

songs and lullabies and eventually loud music and drugs
which maybe I should be taking to overcome this thing
I hardly know how to describe, and which hardly anyone
wants to hear about since who can think too long
about such matters before all they want
is a drink or quiet place to curl up or TV to turn on
along with every light in the house," and when your lover
(if you are lucky enough to have one even if you sometimes
feel bored and stifled by him/her or that maybe you could have
done better especially in terms of having more sex
money complex conversations a heavier plinth
for your nobly woeful statue) asks *What's wrong*
you can forget all this and simply say "I have SAD"
since everyone knows that diagnosis is the first step
though on which stair or ladder is better left unmentioned
since they lead either way, but are best traveled
with someone steadying the rungs or waiting at the top
or bottom with a candle, a word, a cup of something hot
and not too bitter, that you can drink down, and proclaim
good.

# MANNERS

Address older people as *sir* or *ma'am*
unless they drift slowly into your lane
as you aim for the exit ramp.
Don't call anyone *dickhead, fuckface,* or *ass-hat;*
these terms are reserved for ex-boyfriends
or anyone you once let get past second base
and later wished would be sucked into a sinkhole.
Yelling obscenities at the TV is okay,
as long as sports are clearly visible on the screen,
but it's rude to mutter at the cleaning products in Safeway.
Also rude: mentioning bodily functions.
Therefore, sentiments such as "I went balls to the wall for her"
or "I have to piss like a chick with a pelvic disorder at a kegger contest"
are best left unexpressed.
Don't say *chick,* which is demeaning
to the billions of sentient creatures
jammed in sheds, miserably pecking for millet.
Don't talk about yourself. Ask questions
of others in order to show your interest.
How do you like my poem so far?
Do you think I'm pretty?
What would you give up to make me happy?
Don't open your raincoat to display your nakedness.
Fondling a penis in public
is problematic, though Botero's black sculpture
of a fat man, in the Time Warner building
in New York, his pee-pee rubbed gold,
seems to be an exception.
Please lie to me about your pedophilia
and the permafrost layer.

Stay in bed on bad hair days.
When the pulley of your childhood
unwinds the laundry line of your dysfunction,
here is a list of items to shove deep in the dryer:
disturbed brother's T-shirt,
depressed mother's socks and tennis racket,
tie worn by soused father driving the kids home
from McDonald's Raw Bar. If you refuse
your host's offer of alcohol, it is best to say
"I'm so hungover, the very thought of drinking
makes me feel like projectile vomiting,"
or "No thank you, it interferes with my medications."
Hold your liquor whenever it is fearful
and lonely, whenever it needs your love.
Don't interrupt me when I'm battering.
Divorce your cell phone in a romantic restaurant.
Here is an example
of a proper thank-you card:
Thank you for not sharing with me
the extrusions of your vague creative impulse.
Thank you for not believing those lies
everyone spreads about me, and for opening
the door to the next terrifying moment,
and thank you especially for not opening your mouth
while I'm trying to digest my roast chicken.

# WISHBONE

It's bad luck to break a cricket
or a baby, bad to open an evil spirit
in the house or refuse a kiss
if it's offered with a pot of gold.
Better to wear your underpants inside out
on your head, sing at the table,
wet the bed blink years pass
and you stand in a circle passing an apple
from which you can smoke hashish
while your parents sleep
in their bedroom in the next galaxy.
Your fate is written on the stairs
to the rec room and on the doorjamb
where your brothers outgrew you.
You've got a magenta rabbit's foot
on a keychain but no keys yet
to anything, the locks are confusing,
and you may have been misinformed
about rainbows and how to keep lightning
out of the house. Blow out the mirror,
one day it will hate you. Eat a lot
of garlic. When a dog howls,
someone is near. A cat has several lives
and so do you; look, a bird at the window
has eaten your youth but what luck,
all these years later
and you're still a beginner.

# OVER THE BRIGHT AND DARKENED LANDS

# OUT IN THE TRANQUIL BAY

The sea is calm tonight.
Thank you for coming.
It is inoperable.
You are an infidel.
The courtroom is crowded.
The witness has disappeared.
This elixir tastes weird.
The eternal note sounds.
The flatted fifth drones.
Here is your portion.
You are on fire.
Please put yourself out.

# EXCEPT THOU RAVISH ME

Batter my heart.
Burn me with a cigarette.
Show me your dick.
I am fuck-sick.
Knock, knock.
Please break my ribs.
A black eye would be nice.
Your dinner is ready.
The meat is burned.
You drunken pig.
You weak little shit.
That should do it.

# MY SWORD SLEEP IN MY HAND

There's a skunk on the golf course.
Bring me my nine iron.
I can kill the little shit
without raising a divot.
My caddy is an idiot.
My maid is illegal.
My wife's tits sag.
I covet the babysitter.
Bring me my putter.
I own this town.

# AND FEEL THE FELL OF DARK

—*for Juanita*


Sunday and I feel terrible.
The TV says God's been canceled.
I do my grandbaby's braids
by the light of a glass
Jesus candle.
My stove is broken.
My angel is a white woman.
I go out on my porch
smoke a cigarette
and look at the shrine for the girl
who killed herself last week
in the house across the street.
You got to keep
going no matter what
is what I say
today.

# OVER THE BRIGHT AND
# DARKENED LANDS

I sit in one of the dives.
I feel kind of dizzy.
October 29, 2009.
In Peshawar, the shoppers drop.
Explosives in a car
explode kids
and their mothers
in Meena Bazaar.
The bottles look pretty, lit up
like a glass pyre.
There's an olive in my higher power.
The jukebox is haunted.
I brandish my glass.
Smoke stinks in my hair.
We must fuck one another.

# BUT HAVE NOT LOVE

If I lick men, and angels,
they will take me to dinner.
The bells bang all winter.
Angels are picky eaters.
They don't like animals.
Nothing slaughtered
or quartered.
Nothing can be ordered.
Men are a different story;
they chew like cows.
They are easy to kill
because they're blind.
I can see the future
in my burned mirror.
Blacker, and nearer.

# OFF THE BLACK WEST WENT

God climbed into the machine.
Its neon tubes glowed green.

The dials spun
to the sound of violins,

and voilà—God
like a flash fire flared

and vanished
into the face of the deep.

The water was smeared
with great oily

globs of oil.
Meanwhile,

back at the laboratory,
new gizmos were invented

to raise the dead
and bury the living.

Though sometimes, late at night,
a lonely schizophrenic

reading Nietzsche
in the room of his res hotel

was certain he heard a still small roach
calling from under the sink.

# HERE BE
# DRAGONS

# PAREIDOLIA

*(perception of pattern and meaning from
natural randomness)*


The skillet burns that appeared on the tortilla
rolled by Maria Rubio in 1977
looked just like the face of Jesus.
In the bathtub this morning,
a few strands of my hair
formed a wavery peace symbol.
Would you pay to see this miracle?
What about snowflakes—
the cloud they fall from this afternoon
resembles another cloud
which resembles a tennis ball
served by my dead mother in 1947.
Surely that proves that all life on earth
is in a big intergalactic bath towel woven.
Somewhere a snowflake pukes on its shoes
in a convenience store parking lot.
At Jiggles, a half-naked snowflake
pole-dances in panties on the bar.
Across the world, another little snowflake
blows itself up in a crowded café.
Snow everywhere descending.
It gathers to a whiteness.
Why don't we lie down together,
wing-bones touching?
You look like someone I used to love,
only colder.

# INTERNET DATING

I'm tired of kissing nematodes,
splitting the check with scorpions,
listening to the spiritual autobiographies of slugs
over an infinitely repeated series
of banal gestural codes.
I'm thinking of dating trees next.
We could just stand around all night together.
We could stand each other.
I'd murmur, they'd rustle, the wind
would, like, do its wind thing,
without speaking. I hate speech.
Shut up shut up shut up I thought
as he flicked his tongue at the Peruvian tapas,
but the spell didn't work.
Get out of my inbox. I feel violated.
Not in a good way.
There's no one I want to inhale into my alveoli
like I did with you. There, I just made you
into a cigarette. If only
I could press your burning head
into the arrow wound, and twist you, slowly,
to cauterize it. Instead
I want another you, and then another.
You, in the morning after coffee.
Postprandial you. You, especially when I'm drinking.
But back to dating: I don't think I can.
If I read your profile online, I'd never write you.
But I miss all the sides of your face.
I miss the trees of your eyes.
I miss never licking the scar on your hand.

Last night I dreamed you came over
and stayed. If only I could buy
a little property in that dream
and not wake up sick
and freezing, endlessly hitting the return key.

# LOVE POEM (ASSEMBLED FROM FRAGMENTS)

I'll never drink again, swears the alky
on waking, holding the smashed bird of his head
in the frozen ground of his hands. No more cheating,
vows the husband to the hotel showerhead.
Soon the ground will thaw,
the bird shake out its feathers and glide
over the cocktail olives, soon the divorce
cast its spiny shadow over the cell phone bill.
Broken is the cease-fire as dawn fissures
over the barracks, broken the horses
as they're saddled and ridden
into the ruptured trope of sunset.
Everything a shard of the Great Promise
which was sucked into an event horizon
through the first bendable straw
back in prehistory, but still, look
at all the petting zoos, edible panties,
sunflowers growing up through
the rusted-out car at the winery, sutras
penned on torn napkins fluttering
on chain-link fences. Look
at the ROYGBIV of your damp bras,
set out to dry on your dining room table.
They're almost enough but how
much better to encounter one
into which you've been poured.
Behold, thou art flagons of leopards;
thy navel is like a bamboo bong
that wanteth not cannabis,
thy belly is like a sugar glider

set about with crickets and papaya.
Come with me to the cash bar.
I love how you drink your light
like a floater on a transparent 8-Ball,
little triangle pointing to Yes.

# CANDY HEART VALENTINE

In the story of the three little words, things turn out badly:
one is washed overboard, another ends trapped under a machine
drinking and dialing, the third is still apologizing to some rocks.
I've forgotten how to swim, and the sharks are circling. Love
is hopeless in exactly zero of the Hollywood movies I've watched, alone
in bed or else sitting in the overbuttered dark,
someone's hand on my thigh, my hand on someone's stirring
private parts. You were someone to me once, but now I've razored
through most of the frames. I only occasionally hear the clatter
and dying fall before the projector stops. Love according to the Greeks
came in four flavors, *eros* being the most likely to turn to old gum
and so end up smashed on a sidewalk by the boots
and spiked heels of happier passersby, flattened under the swivel
of stroller wheels. You know what I miss? I miss lying next to you
feeling like a lifeboat roped to an ocean liner. Love isn't love,
according to Shakespeare, if it's confused about whether it's a star
or distant satellite, if it's a wine stain that succumbs
to a little seltzer water. You know what else I miss: when you strummed
your electric lyre, its strings flashing in bar light. I still see
a pink cloud where the spill was. Love is deeper than nothing.
You're not here. I' m writing our story in small block letters. LOVE
machine-mixed, stamped into dough. YOU. You know. You know.

# HERE BE DRAGONS

I'm not done with the compass
& I'm still puzzling over the chart
all those squiggles and numbers
sea monsters prowling the depths
devouring ships serpent tusked whale
horsefish finned rhinoceros these
were my lovers these what dragged
me down what I wanted to be taken
to the underwater cities sirens
goatfish sphinxes whores I drank
in the taverns with pirates howler
monkeys my sea captain ancestors my
sozzled staggering fathers & returned
but not to any harbor only the curved
surface I sailed on

# REVIEW OF POSSIBLE SIGNS AND SYMPTOMS

I wonder if it's a problem
that I still believe what I did at five:
my stuffed animals are conscious beings
and love me with their big plastic eyes.
And is it okay that today I can't get to the grocery store?
What about not being able to orgasm
thanks to the drugs that usually help me get to the grocery store—
I should feel worse about that than I actually do.
I probably shouldn't have mentioned the orgasm thing.
There is definitely something wrong with me.
My piston can't connect with my spark plug.
My kitty can't leap to the branch of that tree
the way the squirrel does so easily.
Once I saw one run straight up
the four-story wall of a senior center.
Was that normal? It's normal to start out
as a small, helpless creature and end up
bigger. Cane, walker, wheelchair: pretty standard.
My mother couldn't speak at the end,
only look at me with one dazed eye.
It's normal to cry, lying in bed
with your dying mother. I wonder
if everyone's head sometimes feels
like it's pumped full of Styrofoam pellets.
When I last checked my heart
it was plush and burnt straw.
Should I order a different one
or send it back to the kitchen for reheating?
According to this pamphlet
there are several signs that death is near,

but what about that unmarked stretch of highway
that's been washed away? It's normal to drive
forward slowly in fog and rain, to keep
the radio on for company and love
the disembodied voices saying *Now*
*for a little music, thanks*
*for staying with us, we're going to be here*
*all night long.*

# PROSODY PATHÉTIQUE

Trochees shred your heart to tatters.
Lovers leave you broken, battered.
Fuck you, fuck off: spondees. So what.
Get high. Drop dead. Who cares. Life sucks.
Dactyls are you getting boozed in your underwear,
thinking of someone who used to be there.
These are iambs: *Dolor*. Despair.
And going on and on about your pain,
and sleeping pills, and dark and heavy rain.
Now for the anapests: in the end, you're alone.
In the bag, in the dark, in a terrible rut.
With a smirk, in a wink, the wolves tear you apart.

# FLORIDA

And then there was the man who said "You look fatter
with your clothes off" and like a fool I didn't put them back on
but climbed into his bed beneath the little Tibetan prayer flags
and several images of Buddha haloed by a white light
I wished, at that moment to dematerialize into,
especially when he asked me to get on top, but facing away from him,
so that I rose up and slid down looking at the knees and naked feet
of someone whom, an hour ago, I'd found attractive—in a way, I realized,
it was now a blessing not to have to look into his eyes, but still,
being fucked backwards while facing a stain on the wall that resembled
    Florida
was not quite the encounter I'd envisioned
standing in the bookstore that the Beats with their Blakean visions
and holy passionate excesses had made famous,
and my mind began to wander in order to avoid being present
for whatever was going on down there, eternally, it felt,
and was that really his penis it felt like a speculum
as he groaned and I gazed at Florida thinking of orange groves
and all the nights in Pompano Beach my brothers and I played
    lighthouse tag,
dodging the beam that swept over the black sea and pale sand,
and of all the days I spent shirtless, climbing palm trees or squatting
    with a stick
over a washed-up blue translucent man-o-war quivering in the wind
and of the time I dug a sand pit hoping to trap my crazy violent older
    brother,
anchoring the sharp swords of sticker plants upright in the bottom,
covering the hole with a blanket and just enough sand
and how was I going to lure him in there, maybe I could get him to
    chase me,

he was always chasing me, I could feel my anger
and the great happiness of impending revenge, imagining him falling in,
wishing I could cover him over and bury him forever,
while somewhere in the orange-scented light of a candle
in the universe behind me, my lover finished and I closed my eyes
and never, until now, turned around to look at him
sinking beneath the surface of the bed like a drowning sailor
thrown overboard from a great ship that centuries ago
rounded the Cape and sailed on to another world.

# INVISIBLE SIGNALS

I like it when I forget about time with its cleaning rag
and the drunken gods standing ready with their fly swatters
while I hide in the curtains. I like thinking about the friends I miss,
one with her twenty-four-hour sobriety chip,
one making pozole while her dog
frets in its cage in the kitchen, one helping her sister drag
the oxygen tank to the bathroom. One is preparing her lecture
on the present moment, not mentioning me but here I am,
or was, watching this slut of a river smear kisses all over
east Manhattan, letting the ferries slide under her dress,
her face lit up and flushed. I like to think of my friends
imagining me so we're all together in one big mental cloud
passing between the river and outer space. Here we are
not dissolving but dropping our shadows like darkening
handkerchiefs on the water. One crying by a lake,
one rehabbing her knee for further surgery. One
pulling a beer from the fridge, holding it, deciding.
One calling the funeral home, then taking up
the guitar, the first tentative chord floating out,
hanging suspended in the air.

# THE
# SONNETS

I hate clocks & mirrors I hate all roses
& trees especially trees even evergreens
are felled & strung with lights & ornaments
I hate ornaments & windup crèches
playing "Silent Night" with plastic cows breathing
over a plastic baby I hate babies please don't have one
it will ruin yr beautiful tits forever
you'll have to push a stroller a 40-pound shopping cart
before you like a plow eighteen years you'll toil
what a waste paint something green
get a show somewhere with white walls
& people drinking wine I love wine I love
taking it in my mouth then kissing
it into yours having enough / & time

we went back in the dark singing
I couldn't compare this to anything
I'm not going to talk about it now
sometime too hot the eye of heaven
Cyclops king in the land of the blind
you're too far away please come
every airline fare sometimes declines
it's May in New York still raining
April has a hangover winter was terrible
I didn't sleep last night either
*I don't know how I am*
sorry abt yr fathr call anytime if u need me
Death still has bragging rights
this line has stopped breathing

my glass shall not persuade me I am sober
after three French 75s in the bar mirror
our hair messed up & the bartender
carded us both then look I death my days
but not yet this afternoon it's elsewhere
collecting souls for recycling mine's metallic
scrape the rust off it's still shiny
yours is egg cartons wrapping paper
birthdays weddings congratulations Christmas
mine is Deepest Sympathy Sorry for Your Loss
hearing the champagne hiss in the bottle
& gin to kill the apple maggot
when threatened it walks sideways & mimics a spider
lay down beside you & felt so much older

I hate hearts please don't have one
I wish you wouldn't call me I'm not waiting
by the phone by the light of the clock
in fact I'm really busy right now
describing things that takes a lot of time
you'd be surprised how much drinking
& looking out the window it requires
there's not much room for anything else
all I need is a closet really a little space
for a shoe & I can live on crackers
no problem I love crackers are you eating
some now what do they taste like are you taking
them in your mouth then kissing
my princess I remain your sickening servant

it's that time of year ice in the trees
snow like dirty light piled beside the trash bags
city gardens behind chain-link fences
mired in white except for an occasional rat
everyone lately has cancer
Philip Seymour Hoffman is dead of an overdose
everyone's sad & fascinated
black night is falling in a song
I prefer the one about the glowworm
*illuminate yon woods primeval*
come to bed my aeronautical glimmer
draw a treble clef a few notes will swoop down
nothing lasts anyway
& we leave nothing behind

April again orange tulips in the park strollers
babies acrobats somersaulting
over nervous tourists & jazz quartets
*spiders spinning daydreams*
*I feel so gay in a melancholy way*
enormous artichokes at the farmers' market
kiwis limes asparagus avocados
homesick for their tree their orchard

here is your card The Moon
howling dog & wolf illusions wild rage
we had a Seder & tried to remember the plagues
the dwarfs the deadly sins the seven
people you should never sleep with
the rose inside the rose my artful spring bouquet

let me not to the pediment of two minds
admit marriage; love alter[[[[[[[[[[[[[[[[=[====[[[[[[[[[[[[[[[[[[]

Love is not love
stain remover will take that out

I sd stirred not shaken
I think I'll get a purse dog now it's over

Time + the pussycat O no; O no;
the piggy-wig comes with his sickle

O yes to slay the butcher at last
by the light of the charcuterie, the charcuterie

& every November the turkeys rise like Easter eggs
O their rosy lips & cheeks

your runcible mouth kissing another
I never wrote this nor no woman ever loved

lovely girls doing lines off mirrors;
staying up late with whiskey smoking;
smoldering wavering like TV channels;
in a *Sturm* wind & wreckage rain-wet.

beauties sand in their hair & sheets waking;
with what boy how I'd pluck;
one & then another & what pleasure;
to have them want to ( ) me.

what profuse confusions purposed;
& pulsed going home the next morning;
all that *Drang* I thought was mine;
disappearing the plot the plush design.

( )( )( )( )( )
( )( )( )( )( )

# 130

my mister's eyes are something all right
Mr. Johnson how do you do
his scleras oh they're mighty white
float like a dead man sting like a wound
Captain Crow flew off up some tree
calls me names when Mr. walks with me
burnt roses at the florist stand greening
we went back in the dark singing

oil in a puddle just walk around
oil in the Gulf will slow you down
oil pulled out from deep in de ground
will make a far more pleasing sound
nevertheless when you play your blues
what beauty accrues

damn that was a quick turnaround
now back to the one
gin & tonic the only chord I understand
time to remodel my wounds
when the guitar god looks down
blinding everyone with lightning
building his solo lick by glint
his plectrum flashing his strings all torn
here is my card The Magician
I destroy & redeem I can erase you
from everything but her
did Cyclops have a queen probably not
I'm going to drown both my eyes
my heart already at the bottom of the glass

don't call me at the last minute
I know where you were earlier

the least you could do is deny it
I hate giving up my power this way

I saw you checking out the bartender
talk to me look at me love me kill

the apple maggot when threatened
writes sonnets & is slit down the center

Death is the card it eats the rose down to the core
your black seeds my love my

I hate change & this conversation & you
especially you right now

I'm bleeding all over myself
please fuck me another, please one more thrust

love is my stain no matter what
my red lipstick on your mug
she's married now leave her alone
stop stealing also please stop breathing
maybe I should love you as a friend
it's probably all my fault
but signed sealed I'm yours
then again I'm sick of you
can't we just have a nice Christmas
meal evening birthday spider
restless & sexual isn't everyone
maybe insecurity's the only sin
exhausted & paralyzed
suffocated pitiful fly

champagne hisses in the sickroom
as long as it's bad for you keep drinking it
says my doctor I'm a good patient
no I'm a terrible patient

shake the bottle Little Willie John
Peggy Lee will add words to that song
*Fever with thy flaming youth*
taking it in my mouth then kissing

what was I thinking I wasn't I can't
anymore evermore in a *Sturm* wind
O too late for that, too late, my head
has a hole in it the wind sings through

I thought I died I wrote a fiction
desperate for your black prescription

the Love-god never sleeps never
he falls in flames upon his own arrows
so all the girls feel sorry & O can I have
your baby; sometime too hot
but come on in my kitchen
Mr. Johnson's dead of strychnine
but plenty more biscuits plenty butter
& beans & gravy help yourself
which she did of course
& found a cure for alcoholism & war
good for her but singed sealed I'm no one's
starving breathing sick & by this drowned
came for you yesterday, here you disappear
rinse until the water (will it) (never) runs clear

# THOUSANDS OF TIMES THROUGHOUT THE DAY

# DARKENING, THEN BRIGHTENING

The sky keeps lying to the farmhouse,
lining up its heavy clouds
above the blue table umbrella,
then launching them over the river.
And the day feels hopeless
until it notices a few trees
dropping delicately their white petals
on the grass beside the birdhouse
perched on its wooden post,
the blinking fledglings stuffed inside
like clothes in a tiny suitcase. At first
you wandered lonely through the yard
and it was no help knowing Wordsworth
felt the same, but then Whitman
comforted you a little, and you saw
the grass as uncut hair, yearning
for the product to make it shine.
Now you lie on the couch beneath the skylight,
the sky starting to come clean,
mixing its cocktail of sadness and dazzle,
a deluge and then a digging out
and then enough time for one more
dance or kiss before it starts again,
darkening, then brightening.
You listen to the tall wooden clock
in the kitchen: its pendulum clicks
back and forth all day, and it chimes
with a pure sound, every hour on the hour,
though it always mistakes the hour.

# GIARDINO DEI TAROCCHI, CAPALBIO, ITALY

I'm rearranging the taxidermied rabbit heads
in rows on shelves, riding the streetcar through
the Warsaw Ghetto, swiping my finger over a rose
to change the scenery because this is what you do
in dreams, shake down walnuts from a tree
and dream-feel the *thunk* as one lands on your bare foot.
Real life is mostly a *Blitzkrieg*, one walnut after another
while you head for the shelter. Too bad your town
has an arms factory. Later it will sprout a park but you'll
be *kaput* by then, perchance to create chandeliers
from mummified cats but likely not. So how lucky
to be awake, walking through the gates
of the mosaic city beneath its skyscrapers of women
into a palace of mirrory fractures, surrounded by halflings
with caps and backpacks. Here are The Lovers
picnicking on a rock—bread and wine,
little death face for the avocado pit.
Even Lady Death brimming on her blue horse
is festive. Falling Tower. Magician. Hierophant.
Even the Devil, patron saint of addiction, flanked
by two faceless minions. Even the animal
skulls rigged on a metal contraption, rusted wheel
that drags its chains in the padlocked cell
and creaks scarily, eerily; even that, little ones;
even that.

# REEL

The internist, the neurologist, the gastroenterologist—
Sinemet, Ritalin, Celebrex—
the list written down and lost,
written again and taped to the wall and studied in bewilderment.

Bladder infections, anemia, dizziness, falls.
The husband dead, the house sold.
The trophies gone, and the people who saw the victories.

It sounds like the name of a creature concocted
from electricity and spare body parts,
jerked to ersatz life in a hail of blue sparks:

*Dementia, darling!* the scientist cries
before she fixes him with her burning eyes
and strangles him.

# SLEEP STAGE

In the dream, my mother could again
get out of bed, but only to stand

before a black mirror, so really
not a good dream after all,

and not prescient since the next day
there she still was, bed cranked up,

no teeth, so a kind of swallow hole where
her lips used to be. Into the hole

I maneuvered a spoon of green mush
but then skipped that and the squash

to give her all the pudding,
and went sneaking

to the bathroom to dump the remains
so the nurse wouldn't know. Dreams,

what are they, anyway: collage art,
trash bins, intergalactic interfaces,

maybe random missile fire
from oppressed realities. The blockade

creates a black market, tunnels are dug
to smuggle goats and weapons.

―――――

Dead father laughing at a party.
Ex-lover saving the plane

from crashing into the ice-locked river.
Last night there were lions everywhere

except inside the circle I drew around myself
with a stick in the dirt.

I got into bed with her.
Soon she'll be scattered, probably

over a tennis court somewhere,
which sounds like a dream but won't be.

# NAME THAT MEANS HOLY IN GREEK

## —for Aya

Today I heard your name shouted
by a short-order cook
flipping scallion pancakes in a grease-
grimed Chinese restaurant.
He said it meant *Wow*
which is the best word I know
for the unutterably sublime. *Wow*
is how I had the dumb luck
to become your young and terrified mother
not knowing how to hold you
in the hospital parking lot
while your father got the car.
It seemed to take a long time.
Wow, it seemed to take ten minutes
for you to get your driver's license
and move away to New York.
I remember the moment we made you
and knew we had, your father
lifting himself up off the bed and laughing.
Little hawk, Sumerian goddess,
Kachina that races the wind.
The verses of the Quran are Ayas.
In Japanese, full of color, or beauty,
though once inked for me
as "tomorrow's arrow." The secret
ingredient in the chef's special, a marinade
containing Aya. First word
spoken by a rose, last word the trees

say at night as they lie down
in the forests and fields, last sound
I'll make, if I can still speak at the end,
my palindrome, sword, storm wind.

# ELEGY FOR JON

The lighthouse beam sweeps over me.
I never trusted the sea, always shoving
into coves, scattering salt-glyphs
over tourist hotels, smashing
trawlers and rowboats to sticks. I keep
finding myself beside it, wishing
it would turn into a lake
with maybe a dock floating close to shore.
If not a lake, then a river
between canyons. If not a river
then a big moonlit piano
stocked with fish. *Play irretrievably*
*with the lid closed,*
Satie wrote on one of his scores
but I never discovered which one
or how the music sounded
but this is one way it might go
on a beach where ugly kelp
and a yellowed piano key are flung
from the ocean. I wish the earth
had waited a little longer
before swallowing my brother.
I wish the sea would stop
swallowing his name, while it goes on
kissing the sand, laying
another cold wreath at my feet.

# LOST IN TRANSLATION

Here in Italy I wish someone would explain
a few things like why the dream about the whores
from Algeria and what are those Etruscan markings
on the coffins, and how does it feel to be the hundredth
shorn sheep being herded in a big reverse
question mark across some Umbrian dirt
by a guy in camo pants? It's hard to understand
the woman standing in my room holding towels—
she might be explaining a religious ritual
or how to flush the toilet which maybe amounts
to the same thing if you think of God
as the creator of the toilet and humans
as what comes out of angels after a meal
of scorpions and light. I wonder why the babies
and cherubim in those Renaissance paintings
resemble someone's old drunk uncle
and why all the keychain Pinocchios remind me
of my friend at nine, her stunned look
as we were dropped off at overnight camp. Why
did Dad hide in the clouds, why did Mom lie
about where babies come from? I'm confused
about travel, how the meanings blur
and intersect like tourists and their shadows
as the evening goes quietly insane, mourning
the indifferent sunflowers. Indifference
is the opposite of how Mary gazed upon
her infant son or how I feel
about the sudden rain swirling into the piazza
in front of the Temple of Minerva like
just-poured wine, or maybe like plain water

in a urinal. I wish I understood
this ruined world but then again
why not just be a cobblestone shining
under a sandal, iron griffin creaking from
a hotel awning? The whores were three
and spoke bafflingly in Russian
but all night, whatever they said,
they said it to me.

# DREAM THE NIGHT MY BROTHER DIES

Whichever way I turn there is a door.
I run in and out of the doors.
In one room, inconsolable weeping.
In another, a sad animal regards me.
In a third, a hole in the floor.
I lower my bucket
a long way down on its white rope.

# THOUSANDS OF TIMES THROUGHOUT THE DAY

Oh to be a black-tailed gnatcatcher in the mesquite
gleaning insects from branch-tips with my mate,
our complex song reduced to easy chatter,
our tiny, adorable bodies puffing all blue-gray,
our tails flipping in an expressive way.
Or to walk with a nymph swigging Mike's Hard Lemonade
hand in hand through the bosky suburbs, late
for the stupid party, the dark houses lit
by snow and gaudy crèches, our mouths wet
where they met; and will they meet again? *Not
yet, not yet,* sings the store-bought
animatronic bird. Oh to be thrashing and caught
facedown and fevered on a feathery bed,
or sprawled and scrawled across a page, adored
in ink; to be a glove upon that floor
those bare feet have touched, as my love bends over
to retrieve it. *Not yet, not yet, maybe not ever*
to be part and parcel, pleasured, paired
sings the little robot, geared and levered.
*Here, here,* calls the bird forever.

# WHAT TO SAVE FROM THE FIRE

Grandma offed herself years ago
and the Picasso turns out
to be a pencil drawing
you made at six, triangle of a sail,
duck on a squiggle of water.
Up go the curtains in a bright rush.
You'd definitely save your daughter
and take her place on the pyre,
but she moved to a faraway island
after launching a few thousand ships. -
Once you left a throw rug
on a floor heater to keep the darts
from falling in and woke
to a room made of smoke,
but all that burned was the rug so
it didn't count, the way nothing counted
back then, you and your friends
carrying blankets and pillows outside to sleep
and opening all the windows. Fire is fed
by air, a slim lick of flame expanding
like most people in middle age.
What about your journals—
pages of proof you never changed
no matter what the mirror tells you.
Years from now someone might lick
the ink and taste snow, cheap wine,
the grilled cheeses you ate with your mother
at the Woolworth's counter.
Then again, look at those rosettes of self-pity
adorning the cake of your depression:

let the journals burn. Meanwhile
better wet a towel and hold it to your face.
Who's coming for you? Hopefully large men
in helmets and boots, and not a few students
exhuming a metaphor. Stay calm.
Throw darts. Some look like cruise missiles,
some like honeybees.

# WHITE FLOWER, RED FLOWER

He spent a year playing Death in *La Traviata*,
ruining a camellia in the first act
and smoking a Gauloise in the last
while Violetta succumbed.
Here in the former monastery
the monks succumbed, giving way
to the four of us drinking Sagrantino
and telling stories in the gravel courtyard
under the pasta-shaped stars.
Out in the olive orchard, a mouse
succumbs to a screech owl
and down the hillside, the old painter
who owns this place is yielding,
slowly, to cancer, but today
she recited Montale's poem—
the sunflower crazed with light—
and today we saw the white dog
whose job it is to guide a few sheep
out of Chagall's canvases into the lushness
of the present moment. That moment
has already succumbed to the next
but here we still are, sitting at a small
round table in the dark, drinking
darkness from our glasses,
growing dizzy with darkness,
past midnight now, the date turned over,
date of my friend's birth so more darkness
is poured. In the *chiesa* is a painting
of Jesus emerging from his tomb,
hatted like a Veneto farmer.

In our room is a red-robed Virgin, tiny adult savior
on her lap. A cracked and mottled mirror
on the marble-topped wood bureau,
sepia family portraits on the walls.
*Gran Dio! morir sí giovane,*
sang Pavarotti and Sutherland,
Alfredo and Violetta, she with surprising brio
for someone about to droop, dead,
into her lover's arms. But what difference
your age; everyone's here until
they're not, gone but in some weird
way still hovering in the air,
in a cracked mirror, in the eyes
of those grandparents and great-aunts.
Enter from stage left the red
shock of wings, a disturbance in the trees
easily mistaken for wind.

# THE GIVENS

Someone will bump into you and not apologize, someone will wear
the wrong dress to the party, another lurch drunk into the table
of cheeses and pastries at the memorial service, someone will tell you
she's sorry it's out of her hands as though everything isn't already.
One day the toilet will mysteriously detach its little chain
from its rubber thingy and refuse to flush, in the throes
of whatever existential crisis toilets experience after so much human
waste, so many tampons it wasn't supposed to swallow, so many pills
washed down because someone in a fit of sobriety tossed them in,
     though later
regretted it but too late, they're gone, someone kneeling to empty
a meal, a bottle of wine, too many mango-cucumber-vodka cocktails made
from a recipe by Martha Stewart. Someone will have seen Martha Stewart
in a restaurant, surrounded by admirers. Sinners
will order quail, world leaders stab their forks into small countries
to hold them still for their serrated knives. Ben Franklin said
nothing is certain but death and taxes and he was wrong
about the taxes but then again, right about the impermanency
of the Constitution. No one will come to your door to give you a stack
of bills imprinted with Ben Franklin's face, but a Jehovah's Witness
will find you one day to tell you there is no Hell and that the souls
of the wicked will be annihilated. Someone will love you but not enough,
someone else send gift-wrapped pheromones to your vomeronasal organ
which will promptly destroy them like bugs in a zapper. These are but
     a few
of the many givens, and it's tempting to boil them down to just two
like Franklin did but I prefer Duchamp's *Étants Donnés*,—1. The Waterfall,
2. The Illuminating Gas, water and light, as it was when God began
to pronounce those words in his marble bathroom but given how it's all
gone since then he probably should have skipped the part where clay

sits up and rubs its eyes, looking for something to fuck or kill.
The rain, the lightning. The river town, the fireworks off the dock.
Someone will run through a lawn sprinkler, someone else open a hydrant.
Someone will pull you from the fire, someone else wrap you in flames.

# EULOGY

My mother was a day moon,
my father a missing shoe.
I was born with a stake
in my heart; slowly
it worked its way out
but the last of it remains,
black needle
on the X-ray. I saw God
in a cumulus cloud.
Angels gathered on my library card.
My dog's name was Misty.
I was helpless as a roasted pig
at a wedding. I couldn't tell
my toaster from my ice tray.
My brain had two settings,
puree and liquefy. I grew up
according to legend,
but only a little. Now
I have turned to stone.
Now you can touch me
everywhere.

# ACKNOWLEDGMENTS

*American Poetry Review*: Manners; Sleep Stage; Sonnets 12, 21, 73

*Café Review*: Wishbone

*The Dark Horse* (Scotland): Stray Sparks, Eulogy

*Fifth Wednesday*: Divine

*Five Points*: Introduction to Poetry; Plastic

*Iodine*: Scrapbook; Reel

*Los Angeles Review*: Dream the Night My Brother Dies; Pareidolia

*Mead* (online): Review of Possible Signs and Symptoms

*New Letters*: Applied Mathematics (as Integers)

*Plume* (online): Out in the Tranquil Bay; Over the Bright and Darkened Lands

*Poetry*: Lives of the Poets

*Poetry London* (UK): The Givens

*Poetry Review* (UK): Party; Prosody Pathétique; White Flower, Red Flower

*PoetsArtists*: Ways to Go; Candy Heart Valentine; Giardino Dei Tarocchi

*Psychology Tomorrow* (online): Florida

*River Styx*: Idioms for Rain

*Structo* (UK): Darkening, Then Brightening; Invisible Signals

*Threepenny Review*: What to Save from the Fire

*Virginia Quarterly Review*: Except Thou Ravish Me

*Willow Springs*: Internet Dating

"Divine" also appeared in *Best American Poetry 2013*. "Darkening, Then Brightening" was also a selection for Poem-A-Day from the Academy of American Poets.

Gratitude: Jill Bialosky, Donna Masini, and Rob McQuilkin. Thanks to the Civitella Ranieri Foundation and La Romita School of Art for time and inspiration.

## ABOUT THE AUTHOR

Kim Addonizio is the author of six previous poetry collections including *Tell Me*, a finalist for the National Book Award. Her other books include a memoir, *Bukowski in a Sundress* (Viking/Penguin), two novels, two story collections, and two books on writing poetry: *The Poet's Companion* (with Dorianne Laux) and *Ordinary Genius: A Guide for the Poet Within*. Addonizio has received numerous honors for her work including two NEA Fellowships, a Guggenheim Fellowship, and Pushcart Prizes in both poetry and the essay. She plays harmonica with the word/music group Nonstop Beautiful Ladies, has released two word/music CDs, and is an occasional presenter for BBC Radio. She also teaches private poetry workshops and volunteers for The Hunger Project, a global organization empowering impoverished people to achieve self-reliance. Visit her online at www.kimaddonizio.com.